ORIGIN OF *Life*
Teacher Supplement

ORIGIN OF *Life*

TEACHER SUPPLEMENT

INSTITUTE for CREATION RESEARCH

SCIENCE EDUCATION ESSENTIALS is a curriculum supplement series designed to cover vital topics in the various science disciplines, all from a thoroughly biblical viewpoint. Each product includes a teacher instructional guide, along with K-12 activities and classroom helps to guide discussion, reinforce subject content, and facilitate hands-on laboratory exercises.

Published by the Institute for Creation Research.

SCIENCE EDUCATION ESSENTIALS

Series Creator:	Dr. Patricia L. Nason Chair, Science Education Department, ICR Graduate School
Project Manager:	Janis McCombs
Managing Editor:	Beth Mull
Graphic Designer:	Susan Windsor
Science Reviewers:	Dr. John Morris, Dr. Charles McCombs, Dr. Jeff Tomkins, Dr. Randy Guliuzza, Dr. Chris Osborne, Dr. Larry Vardiman, Dr. Tim Clarey, Brian Thomas, Frank Sherwin

ISBN: 978-0-932766-96-0

ORIGIN OF LIFE

Teacher Supplement Author:

Dr. Daniel C. Criswell received his Ph.D. from the University of Montana in biochemistry with an emphasis in molecular biology. While at the University of Montana, Dr. Criswell researched the effects of mutations on bacteria and taught introductory biology. He earned a master's degree in biology from the Institute for Creation Research Graduate School, where he studied the effects of mutations on hair development in rats and helped develop the Good Science curriculum with Dr. Richard Bliss. Dr. Criswell has published several papers on the effects of mutations and DNA degradation in bacteria, mammals, and humans.

Dr. Criswell has extensive teaching and curriculum development experience. He was a high school biology teacher for 15 years in Oregon and Montana, in addition to his teaching experience at the University of Montana and the ICR Graduate School. He has written science curriculum materials for ages K-12 for use in homeschool workshops, as well as for teachers in Christian schools. Many of the activities that accompany this book were originally presented at ICR Good Science workshops for Christian schools and homeschool parents.

K-12 Instructional Contributors: Dr. Daniel Criswell, Dr. Patricia Nason, Dr. Charles McCombs, Janis McCombs, Leona Criswell

For additional resources from the Institute for Creation Research, please visit www.icr.org or call 800.337.0375.

Copyright © 2009 by the Institute for Creation Research. All rights reserved. No portion of this book may be used in any form without written permission of the publisher, with the exception of brief excerpts in articles and reviews. For more information, write to Institute for Creation Research, P. O. Box 59029, Dallas, TX 75229.

ISBN: 978-0-932766-97-7

Printed in the United States of America.

PREFACE

Teachers mold the minds of their students, helping them construct knowledge and an understanding of the world around them. A teacher's influence on the belief system, as well as cognitions, of a student can affect the student for a lifetime.

For nearly 40 years, the Institute for Creation Research has equipped teachers with evidence of the accuracy and authority of Scripture. In keeping with this mission, ICR presents Science Education Essentials, a series of science teaching supplements that exemplifies what ICR does best—providing solid answers for the tough questions teachers face about science and origins.

This series promotes a biblical worldview by presenting conceptual knowledge and comprehension of the science that supports creation. The supplements help teachers approach the content and Bible with ease and with the authority needed to help their students build a defense for Genesis 1-11.

Each science teaching supplement includes:

- A content book written at the high school level to give teachers the background knowledge necessary to teach the concepts of scientific creationism with confidence. Each content book is written and reviewed by creation scientists, and can be purchased separately in class sets.

- A CD-ROM packed with teacher resources, including K-12 reproducible activities and PowerPoint presentations. The instructional materials have been pilot tested for ease in following instructions and completeness of activities. They have also been reviewed by scientists for scientific accuracy and by theologians for biblical correctness.

Science Education Essentials are designed to work within a school's existing curriculum, with an uncompromising foundation of creation-based science instruction. Secular textbooks are finding their way into Christian schools. Teachers may not lack belief in the Word of God, but they often do not have adequate information or knowledge concerning the tenets of scientific and/or biblical creation. Science Education Essentials equips teachers with the tools they need to teach the science of origins from a biblical rather than an evolutionary worldview.

The goal of each science supplement is to:

a) increase the teacher's understanding of and confidence in scientific creation and the truth of God's Word, while glorifying God as Creator;

   But sanctify the Lord God in your hearts: and be ready always to give an answer to every man that asketh you a reason of the hope that is in you with meekness and fear. (1 Peter 3:15)

b) provide teachers with a toolkit of activities and other instructional materials that build a foundation for their students in creation science apologetics;

Beware lest any man spoil you through philosophy and vain deceit, after the tradition of men, after the rudiments of the world, and not after Christ. (Colossians 2:8)

c) encourage the use of the higher level thinking necessary to stand firm against the lies of evolution and humanism.

…that we henceforth be no more children, tossed to and fro, and carried about with every wind of doctrine, by the sleight [trickery] of men, and cunning craftiness, whereby they lie in wait to deceive; but speaking the truth in love, may grow up into him in all things, which is the head, even Christ. (Ephesians 4:14-15)

With Science Education Essentials, teachers can equip the future generation of scientists and individuals to examine the evidence for the truth of Scriptures through an understanding of creation science. By using hands-on activities and relating scientific truth to the Bible, teachers/parents will be grounding their children in creation science truths so they can provide a logical response when challenged with science that is based on a philosophy that is in direct contradiction to Genesis 1-11.

As the leading creation science research organization, ICR is providing meaningful creation science material for classroom use. Our desire is that the materials renew minds, defend truth, and transform culture (Romans 12:1-2) for the glory of the Creator.

Dr. Patricia L. Nason
Science Education Department Chair
Institute for Creation Research Graduate School

Table of Contents

	PAGE
What is the Origin of Life?	9
What is Life?	11
A Physical Definition of Life	11
A Biblical Definition of Life	13
The Chemical Basis for Physical Life	17
Physical Life Requires Catalysts, Information, and Metabolism	17
The Elements for Life Came from the Earth	18
Enzymes Catalyze the Reactions that Make Life Possible	19
DNA Is the Information Storage System for Life	22
Metabolic Cycles Are Characteristic of Life	25
Creating Life in the Laboratory	29
Amino Acids in the Prebiotic Soup	30
"The RNA World"	32
The Metabolism First Hypothesis	34
Does Life Exist Somewhere Else in the Solar System?	37
Life on Mars?	37
Stanley Miller's Chemistry on Titan	40
The Purpose of Creation	41
Bibliography	45

What is the Origin of Life?

Have you seen the surface of Mars recently? Pictures of the Martian surface appear regularly on television, and in magazines and newspapers. These pictures were taken by National Aeronautics and Space Administration (NASA) space probes that landed on the surface of Mars to sample the contents of Martian rocks and soil. Not only did the probes take pictures and sample the soil, but video cameras recorded dust devils blowing across the plains and lasers detected falling snow. The surface of Mars is completely barren and looks very different from any place on earth. Even most deserts on earth have a few plants and animals clinging to life, while many other places have an abundance of life.

How did life get started on earth? Many scientists believe that life began from natural processes that did not require any supernatural acts. Scientists have done many experiments to understand how the first molecules, important for life, could organize themselves into living things by natural processes. These experiments led many scientists to conclude that the earth's current atmosphere and surface do not favor the formation of the first molecules necessary for life. Were the conditions on earth when life began different from what they are now? Was life brought to earth from another place in the solar system or galaxy? In addition to the results of laboratory experiments, many scientists believe the key to understanding how life started on earth begins by investigating the conditions found on other planets in our solar system. They think that perhaps the other planets will provide clues for how life formed from nonliving material.

A Martian landscape.
Image Credit: NASA/JPL

ORIGIN OF LIFE

An alternative explanation for how life began on earth comes from the Bible. The Bible tells us that God spoke the earth into existence and then formed living things from the elements of the earth. The account of creation in Genesis 1 indicates that God created living things fully formed. The creation account eliminates the need to discuss which molecules came first, or which biological systems came first, since all of them were created when "life as we know it" was created. The creation account can appropriately be termed a miracle since only God can create life simply by speaking it into existence. However, what was created and how it functions is observable and therefore not outside the realm of science. Science can be defined as simply investigating the nature of God's creation and how it works. Life's dependency on fully-formed living systems and living things can be observed and tests can be made to determine the extent of the dependency. For example, different forms of life are dependent on other forms of life. Some plants are dependent on insects for pollination, and many insects are dependent on specific plants for food. Life's dependence on fully functional systems, whether a biochemical pathway in a cell or a healthy ecosystem, is evidence that life was created fully formed and functional.

What is Life?

A Physical Definition of Life

We know life when we see it, but how do we define it? Even a child understands that an ant creeping down the sidewalk is alive, while the pebbles on the sidewalk are not. The free movement of the ant is a "dead" giveaway that it is significantly different from the immobile pebbles. Unfortunately, this simple definition of life based on locomotion does not include all life forms, since the leafy tree next to the sidewalk is alive also, but not moving on its own. Life has many different qualities, making it difficult to define precisely.

Scientists have defined life in several different ways, with most of the definitions emphasizing what living things do. However, all living things have one physical trait in common: they are made of cells. There are living things that have only one cell, referred to as one-celled plants (e.g., algae) and animals (e.g., amoebas), and living things with trillions of cells, like people, animals, and trees. All of life's functions are the result of the activity that takes place in cells. Cells make the heart beat, provide chemicals for digestion, and contract to allow an animal to move muscles, to name just a few of their functions. Cells are the basic units of physical life.

The physical life of an organism can be partially defined by movement, reproduction and growth, responsiveness, and the use of energy. Movement includes more than the mobility of an organism such as an ant. Remember, the tree next to the sidewalk is also alive, but it is not capable of locomotion like the ant. The tree provides us with an expanded definition of movement. Movement includes moving substances inside a living thing. The tree is capable of moving substances inside the trunk, roots, and leaves. Sugars formed from photosynthesis can be transported from the leaves to the roots, and water from the roots can be transported to the leaves.

Reproduction is another function of living things. We usually think of reproduction in the context of a dog having puppies or the arrival of a baby sister or brother, but reproduction also includes the ability of living things to reproduce new cells. As the cells in any living thing wear out and die, more cells must be reproduced to replace them. If the number of cells produced exceeds the number of cells that are lost, the living thing grows. We typically associate growing with getting taller, but it can also include growing leaves, flowers, fingernails, and a host of other structures. (Some of us would rather not think about adding any more cells to our bodies and growing larger!)

Origin of Life

Living things respond to stimuli in the environment. Animals have a brain and sensory organs that enable them to respond to stimuli that they see, hear, feel, and smell. Plants are also capable of responding to the environment, even though they lack the brain and sensory organs found in animals. The first stems to emerge from a plant seed, and ultimately the trunk of a tree, will grow away from gravity and towards sunlight, while the roots do the opposite. Many plants are able to respond to the length of daylight, with some plants flowering when the days are long and some when the days are short. Even microscopic bacteria respond to chemical changes in their environment. These responses can lead bacteria to food or to similar bacteria to form colonies or "films."

To accomplish the various activities listed above, all living things must use energy. Energy is acquired from the food that many living things eat or ingest. Some living things, like green plants, acquire their energy through photosynthesis, a process that converts light energy into chemical energy stored in sugars. Living things change their environment by taking in substances to produce energy and then releasing the waste products from this activity. This is most easily illustrated by the air that is exhaled from an animal or from humans. Carbon dioxide is a waste product from the breakdown of food molecules in our cells. We exhale air that contains 100 times more carbon dioxide than atmospheric air contains. Our breathing changes the amount of carbon dioxide that is in the air in our immediate surroundings.

Living things also use energy to make substances, which decreases the entropy within their cells, while the release of waste material increases entropy outside of the cells. Entropy is simply a measurement for disorder or randomness. If entropy increases, there is an increase in randomness; if entropy decreases, there is a decrease in randomness. Cells use energy to make larger substances out of smaller subunits. Building larger structures from smaller subunits decreases the entropy, or randomness, in the cell. This is analogous to building a house from a pile of wood.

There is more randomness in a pile of wood than in the orderly building of a house. A decrease in entropy within a cell is typically accompanied by the release of waste products from the cell into its surroundings. The release of waste products (such as carbon dioxide broken down from sugar) into the surroundings would increase the entropy of the surrounding environment. Therefore, a change in entropy is observed in the environment due to the use of energy by living things. There is a decrease in entropy in the cell and an increase in entropy outside the cell. The change in entropy is one way to detect the presence of living things that cannot be easily seen.

It could be argued that an automobile also changes the environment by producing energy from the combustion (burning) of gasoline. The car exhaust changes the immediate environment by giving off carbon monoxide in quantities large enough to harm any living thing near it. However, the automobile does not have the other qualities of life that were discussed above. Just like the example of the tree and locomotion, an incomplete definition of what life is will not identify all life forms and might identify an object as living when it is not.

A Biblical Definition of Life

How does the Bible define life? Is there anything significantly different between a physical definition of life and what the Bible has to say about living things? Are there any significant differences between plant, animal, and human life?

Plants were created on day three of the creation week. We are told in Genesis 1:11 that God brought forth plants from the earth. This is consistent with the observation that plants are made of the same elements that are commonly found in the earth. In Genesis 1:30, we are told that plants were created to provide food for animals and humans. Plants perform all of the functions identified with physical life. They can move, reproduce and grow, respond to the environment, and use energy. Plants are marvelously complex reproducing or replicating systems that are capable of growing in a variety of habitats and producing a large variety of foods for life on earth. Most plants are capable of producing fruit or other reproductive structures, such as pine cones, that can be removed without harming the plant. Certainly, picking fruit off a plant will not cause it to die. There are no further comments in Scripture concerning the nature of life in plants. They are representatives of life, brought into existence by the word of God, exhibiting only the physical nature of life.

Other living things that are obvious replicating systems include fungi, bacteria, and one-celled plants and animals. Although many of these cannot be described as green plants, they are necessary for providing food for animals and humans by recycling nutrients back through nature, or for assisting animals and humans to digest nutrients.

During the fifth and sixth days of creation (Genesis 1:20-25), God created animals and humans. Animals, like plants, were created from the elements commonly found in the earth. Animal life can also be defined by the physical qualities of what living things do. However, animals are described as "living creatures," giving them a different quality from plant life. The Hebrew word for "living" in this passage can be translated as "soul," indicating that the nature of life in an animal is distinct from

Origin of Life

that in plants. The term "soul" has frequently been used as a synonym in the English language for the human spirit, which is eternal. This is not what is meant when animals are identified as living creatures. The Bible does not teach that animals have an eternal spirit or soul. Animals have a "soul," indicating they have consciousness, not an eternal spirit. We might further define this as awareness, or animate behavior. However we define this, it is obvious from the passage that animals were created with a different quality, a consciousness or awareness, that plants lack. This quality can be observed in the behavior of many animals.

Plants and animals were created for a different purpose, which is reflected in their structure and function. Plant cells are distinctly different from animal cells, making plants quite different from animals in appearance. Animals are characterized by locomotion, the ability to move from one place to another, unlike plants such as trees, shrubs, and grasses, which are not capable of moving from one place to another. Plants are able to make food, using the sun as an energy source and carbon dioxide from the air to build sugar molecules. Animals and humans must eat and digest food for their nutrients, which is why God provided green plants as a source of food. The physical differences in plants and animals provide a reminder that they were created for different purposes, with animals possessing a quality, consciousness, not given to plants.

Humans, like the plants and animals, were created from the elements of the earth ("dust of the earth," Genesis 2:7). Man is described as a "living being" (Genesis 2:7). Like the animals, "living being" is translated here from the same Hebrew word for "soul." Again the term "soul" refers to the consciousness and self-awareness that humans possess and does not equate the eternal spirit in humans with animals. We get more information about what it means to be a "living being" or "living creature" from the creation of humans. Man was made a living being when God breathed the "breath of life" into him, indicating that this form of life comes directly from God. Genesis 7:15 identifies animals as having the "breath of life," confirming that they share a living quality with man.

In addition to being given a physical body and becoming a living being, man was created in the "image of God," making him distinctly different from plants and animals. There are many facets of God's image that can be seen in humans, which are not necessary to describe in this book. It is sufficient to note that God is "spirit" (John 4:24) and being created in God's image gives man a "spirit," which to some degree reflects God's nature and has the potential to live eternally in the presence of God or eternally separated from God. "Spirit" is frequently used interchangeably with the word "soul" to describe humans. Man was created with a spirit, sometimes referred to as the soul, that requires salvation. This spirit, and the need for salvation, distinguishes man from the other forms of life God created. A summary of the life in man can be understood from Christ's commandment to "love the Lord thy God with all thy heart [physical life], and with all thy soul [spiritual life], and with all thy mind [consciousness]" (Matthew 22:37).

To summarize, there are three different aspects, or levels, of life given in the Bible. Living things can have physical life, conscious life, and/or spiritual life. Physical life can be defined by what living things are made from and by what they do. All life forms on earth share this quality, and it is a quality that can easily be studied in the laboratory. A second level of life is animate or conscious life. Animals and humans are described as living creatures or beings having a consciousness ("soul" or mind). The third aspect of life is the spirit. Only man was created in God's image, giving him spiritual life.

The Bible clearly states that the origin of life resulted from the spoken word of God. The elements necessary for physical life came into existence and plants were formed from the earth by the spoken word of God. Animals and humans were also commanded by God's word to form. Man became a living being when God breathed the breath of life into him. All life came from pre-existing life and from an intelligent source that made systems to sustain that life. The Bible tells us that God is the origin of life.

The Chemical Basis for Physical Life

We observe that all life comes from similar pre-existing life—a concept termed biogenesis. This includes the smallest bacteria to the largest mammals and dinosaurs. If life comes from pre-existing life, then life must have come from an eternal life source in the beginning. The God of the Bible is identified as this eternal life source. If God is not the source of life, then life came into existence by some other means. Scientists who do not believe that a god created life are forced to provide an alternative explanation. This has led to many hypotheses, experiments, and space missions to find clues for how life could have come into existence from nonliving sources.

Scientists who reject a god as the origin of life theorize that life originated from the molecules that are found in living things. These molecules would theoretically organize themselves into chemical pathways to produce information and energy to sustain the reactions necessary for physical life. Many of the experiments designed to show how life could have come into existence from nonliving sources simply reinforce the concept that an intelligent source, the God of the Bible, is required for life as we know it.

Physical Life Requires Catalysts, Information, and Metabolism

How do the molecules necessary for life carry out the functions that make life possible? If we assemble the correct chemistry into a membranous sack, similar to a living cell, does that constitute a living thing? What else is required besides the right chemistry to make something alive? The chemistry of living things enables them to move, respond, reproduce and grow, and use energy. Three of the most important factors that make living things work and separate them from non-life are: 1) a catalyst that controls the rate of chemical reactions necessary for life; 2) an information system to regulate these reactions that has the ability to pass information on to the next generation of reactions, cells, or organisms; and 3) a metabolic system to provide an energy source to make chemical reactions useful. These systems come from the organization of the chemistry in living systems.

The Elements for Life Came from the Earth

Were living things made from the elements in the earth? In Genesis 1:11, God commanded the land to produce vegetation, and in Genesis 1:24, He said for the land to produce living creatures, indicating that God made living things right from the elements in the earth. Even man was created from the "dust of the ground" (Genesis 2:7). All scientists agree that living things are made from the same elements found in the soil and rocks of the earth. Carbon, hydrogen, oxygen, and nitrogen are the most common elements found in living things, with lesser amounts of sulfur, phosphorous, calcium, potassium, and a few other elements also present. These are all elements commonly found in the earth.

Element	Symbol	% of Human Body by Weight	% of the Earth Crust by Weight
Oxygen	O	65.0	46.6
Carbon	C	18.5	0.03
Hydrogen	H	9.5	0.14
Nitrogen	N	3.3	trace
Calcium	Ca	1.5	3.6
Phosphorous	P	1.0	0.07
Potassium	K	0.4	2.6
Sulfur	S	0.3	0.03
Silicon	Si	trace	27.7
Aluminum	Al	trace	6.5
Iron	Fe	trace	5.0

The most common elements in the human body are also found in the earth. Trace elements are less than 0.01% of the total.

Physical life is based on the chemistry of carbon and the molecules it forms. Carbon is capable of forming four covalent bonds with the other elements commonly found in living creatures. Covalent bonds are formed when carbon, oxygen, hydrogen, nitrogen, and other nonmetals share electrons. These covalent bonds form molecules vital to the chemistry of life. Water (H_2O), an important solvent for living systems, is also formed by covalent bonding.

Origin of Life

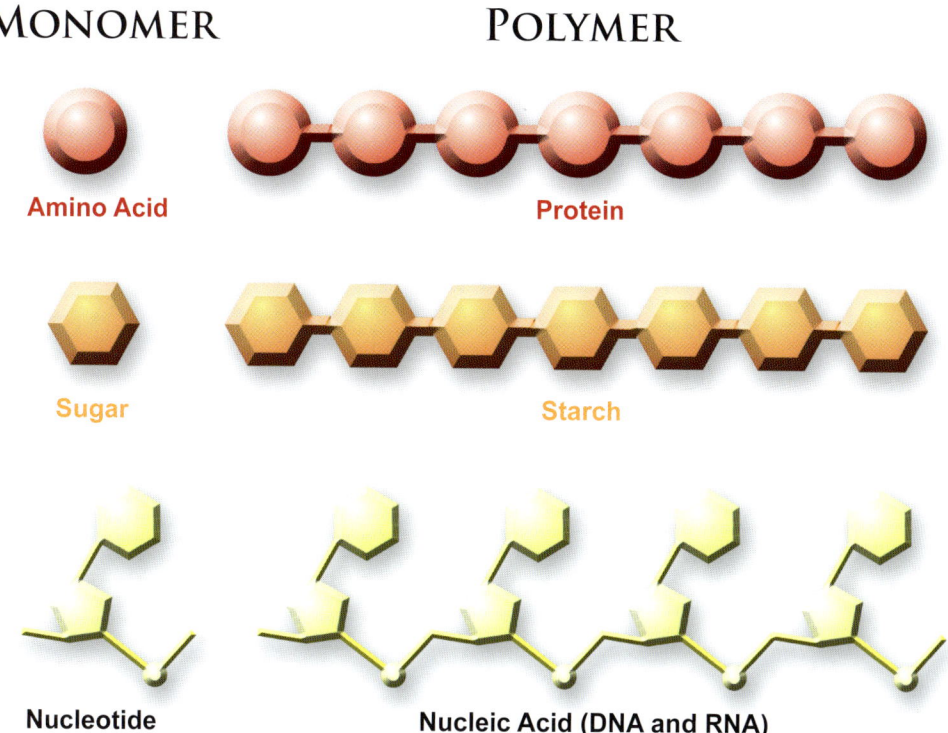

The molecules of life form long chains or polymers from subunits or monomers.

Carbon-based molecules form many different types of molecular chains. The long molecular chains formed from carbon-based molecules are called polymers (many units) that are bonded together from monomers (one unit). These monomers form polymers in a way that is similar to how individual beads on a string form a necklace. Not only do these molecules form chains, but these chains can have branches, form coils or spirals similar to bed springs and staircases, or form large globular molecules. There are three types of polymers found in living things and all of them have carbon, hydrogen, and oxygen in various amounts. These three polymers are proteins, carbohydrates, and nucleic acids. Proteins are formed from amino acid monomers. Amino acids have nitrogen in addition to carbon, hydrogen, and oxygen, and two amino acids, methionine and cysteine, have sulfur. Carbohydrates, or starches, are formed from sugars. The nucleic acids, DNA and RNA, are formed from nucleotides. Nucleic acids have nitrogen and phosphorous in addition to carbon, hydrogen, and oxygen. A fourth type of molecule important for living systems is lipids. Lipids are formed from fatty acids and are one of the main components of cell membranes, a topic not covered in this book.

Enzymes Catalyze the Reactions that Make Life Possible

Proteins that catalyze life-dependent reactions are called enzymes. Enzymes control the rate of chemical reactions. Many chemical reactions necessary for life are not spontaneous and do not occur quickly enough

Origin of Life

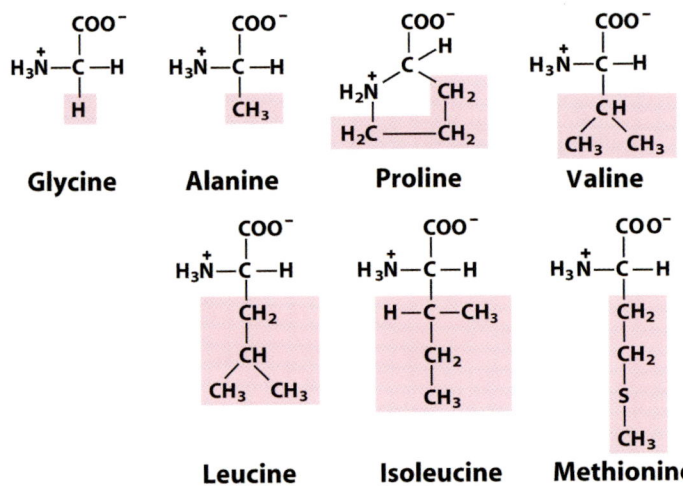

The structure of several amino acids. The amine group is on the left and the carboxyl group is at the top of each molecule. Each amino acid is determined by the "R" group, which is highlighted in pink.

to benefit a living thing. Enzymes provide the catalyst necessary to make chemical reactions occur at a rate that is beneficial to life. This is easily understood by considering the digestive system of animals. The food that an animal consumes will not break down fast enough on its own into the nutrients necessary to benefit the animal. Enzymes speed up the process of breaking down food substances so the animal will acquire nutrients at a fast enough rate to continue living. Each enzyme reacts with a specific substance or substrate. The structure of an enzyme that enables it to react with a specific substrate is determined by its sequence of amino acids.

Amino acids, the subunits of proteins, are identified by a central carbon bonded to an amine (NH_2) and a carboxyl (COOH). In addition to these two bonds, the central carbon is bonded to a hydrogen atom (H) and what is called a side chain or "R" group. The "R" group is different in each amino acid and determines the chemical properties of each. Some amino acids have several carbons arranged in a chain for an "R" group, while the amino acid glycine has just hydrogen for an "R" group. Amino acids are bonded together when the amine group (NH_2) of one amino acid forms a peptide bond with the carboxyl group (COOH) of a second amino acid. Many amino acids bonded together form a polymer, or polypeptide. A functional polypeptide in a cell is called a protein. Proteins in living things are formed from 20 different amino acids into molecules that typically have 200-2,000 amino acids, although the number of amino acids in a protein can vary from 51 (insulin) to thousands. Different proteins and their functions are determined by the sequence of amino acids and the protein shape they produce. Portions of proteins can assume a myriad of shapes, including coils and pleated sheets that look like curtains.

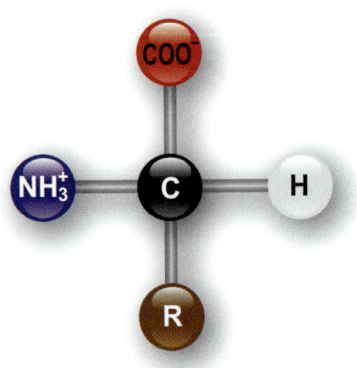

An illustration of an amino acid showing the four bonds that carbon can form with other atoms. Carbon can form up to four covalent bonds with other nonmetals. The "R" stands for any other atom at this bonding site.

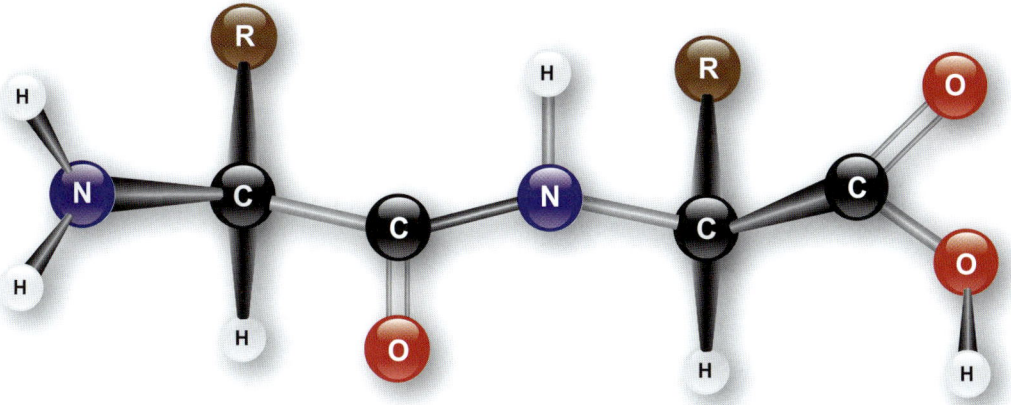

The peptide bonds between several amino acids forming a polypeptide. "R" groups of individual amino acids are highlighted in red.

Amino acids in living things are left-handed molecules, with the rare exception of a few right-handed amino acids in antibiotics and in the cell walls of bacteria. There are several methods of determining "handedness," but in amino acids it is based on the arrangement of the molecules that are bonded to the central or chiral carbon. When carbon bonds to four different atoms or molecules, it is asymmetrical and is called a chiral carbon. Left-handed amino acids are typically illustrated with the amine group (NH_2) on the left and the carboxyl group (COOH) on the right. All amino acids are chiral except for glycine, which does not have four different atoms bonded to the central carbon. The chirality of amino acids is characteristic of living chemistry and identifies the presence of living things, while the lack of chirality is characteristic of nonliving chemistry. The specificity of only left-handed amino acids in living things is strong evidence that life did not arise from nonliving processes, but instead was designed and created.

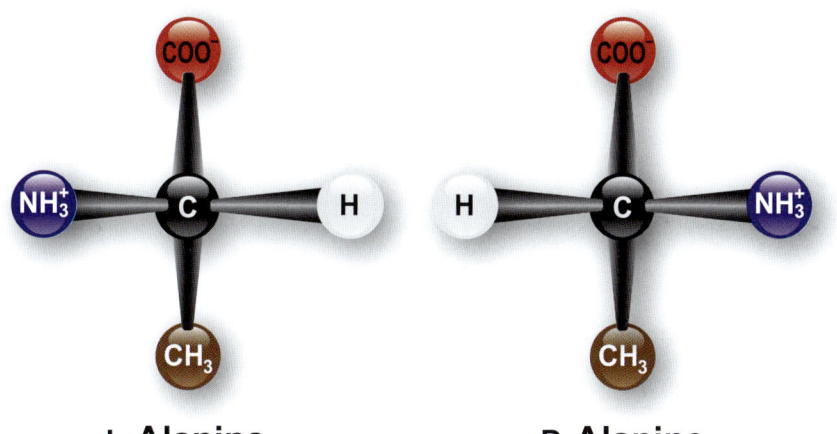

L-Alanine   D-Alanine

The structure of left- and right-handed alanine. The amine group is written on the left. The "R" group, CH_3, distinguishes alanine from other amino acids. There are four different groups, COO-, NH_3^+, H, and CH_3, bonded to the central carbon, making this a chiral carbon. The molecule is three dimensional, with H and NH_3^+ in front of the chiral carbon while COO- and CH_3 are behind the chiral carbon.

ORIGIN OF LIFE

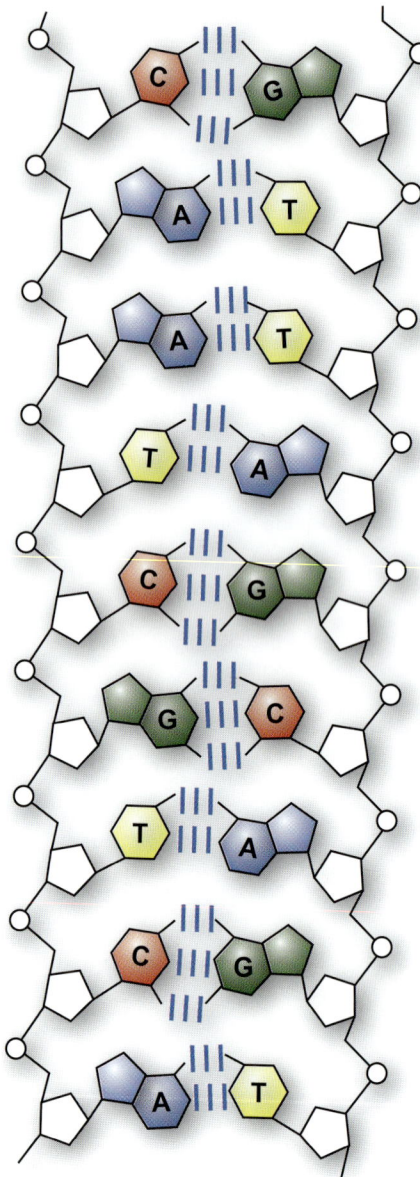

DNA is the Information Storage System for Life

Many substances, such as proteins, are made from the activity of more than one enzyme. Many components necessary for life are produced from the activities of a series of reactions catalyzed by several different enzymes. To produce these substances at the right time and in the right amount, an information system is needed. This information system coordinates and regulates the manufacture of proteins or the breakdown of food substances. In addition to regulating the chemical reactions necessary for life, information has to be stored and replicated (duplicated) to provide instructions for the activities of the next generation of cells or organisms (living things).

Deoxyribonucleic acid (DNA) is the molecule that coordinates and regulates the chemical reactions that make life possible, and it stores this information for the next generation. DNA is formed from the arrangement of subunits called nucleotides, with each nucleotide consisting of three components; a sugar (deoxyribose), phosphate group, and base. Nucleotides are the monomers, or subunits, that form the DNA polymer. DNA is a double-stranded molecule with sugar-phosphate molecules forming the strands and bases that are hydrogen-bonded to each other to hold the two strands together. A DNA molecule has the shape of a spiral staircase, with the base pairs forming the steps, and the sugar-phosphate "backbone" forming the sides.

Double-stranded DNA. The bases are paired according to the number of hydrogen bonds that can be formed between them. Adenine and thymine share two hydrogen bonds, while cytosine and guanine share three hydrogen bonds. Each hydrogen bond is represented with three dashed lines. The order of bases in DNA determines what the living thing will be and what substances will be produced.

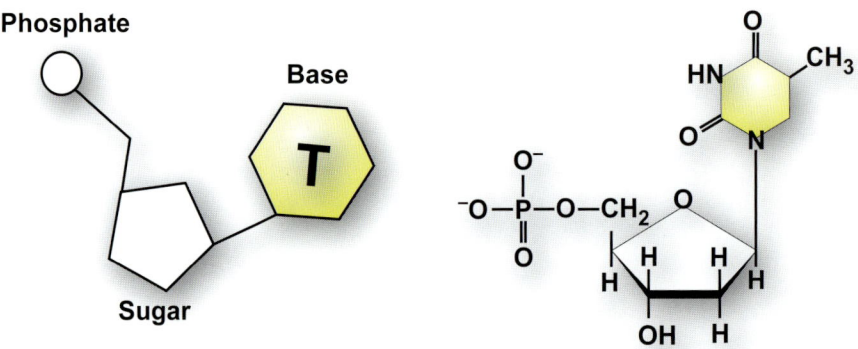

A DNA nucleotide with thymine as the nitrogen base.

Origin of Life

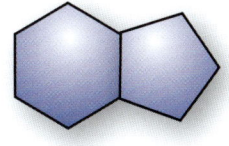 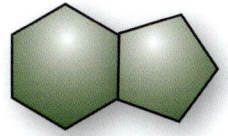  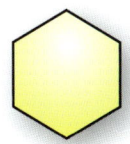

Adenine   **Guanine**   **Cytosine**   **Thymine**

The four nitrogen bases in DNA. Cytosine and thymine have one ring and are called pyrimidines. Adenine and guanine have two rings and are purines. Adenine pairs with thymine, and cytosine with guanine in double-stranded DNA.

A nucleotide can have one of four different bases: adenine, guanine, thymine, or cytosine covalently bonded to the sugar (deoxyribose). These bases are "ring-shaped" structures that have several nitrogen atoms. Cytosine and thymine have just one ring, while adenine and guanine have two rings. Each base has a specific base partner. Adenine, on one side of the double-stranded DNA molecule, bonds to thymine on the other side, while cytosine bonds to guanine in the same manner. The bonds formed between the bases are hydrogen bonds that are considerably weaker than the covalent bonds that form the nucleotides. This is an important feature. Sections of the double-stranded DNA (called genes) have to be able to separate into two strands so that the information in DNA can be transcribed into a messenger in the form of ribonucleic acid (RNA). Because the hydrogen bonds are much weaker than covalent bonds, it takes less energy to separate them and the energy released does not adversely affect the covalent bonds holding the nucleotides together on each strand of DNA.

The information in DNA is stored in the order, or arrangement, of the different nucleotides. The order of these four bases in DNA "spell out" the instructions necessary to maintain life, much the same way letters spell out words in a sentence. With the help of many enzymes and a few energy molecules, DNA can tell the cells of living things which proteins to make and how much. It can even provide information about how long the protein is to last in the cell. DNA also responds to environmental cues and will replicate, or copy itself, to provide essentially identical DNA for the next generation of cells. This is part of the process that makes reproduction possible for living things.

There is another nucleic acid in living things called ribonucleic acid, or RNA. It has the same basic structure as DNA, being made of nucleotides composed of a phosphate, sugar, and four different bases. There are essentially two differences between RNA and DNA. RNA nucleotides have the sugar ribose, while DNA has the sugar deoxyribose, and the base uracil is utilized in RNA instead of the DNA base thymine. Many

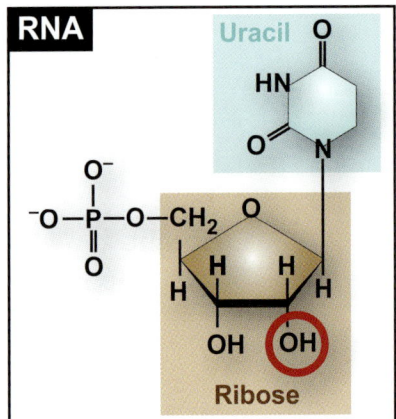 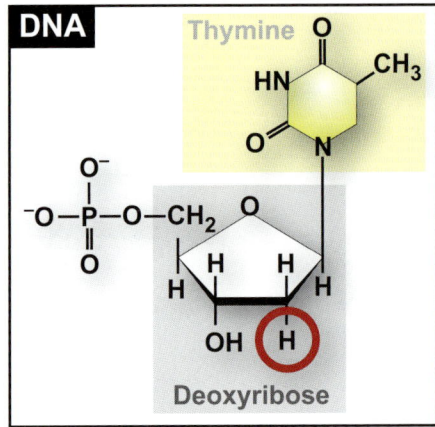

The RNA nucleotide uracil compared to the DNA base thymine. RNA has the sugar ribose, while DNA has the sugar deoxyribose. The only difference in the two sugars is the loss of oxygen in deoxyribose. The RNA base uracil pairs with adenine in place of the DNA base thymine.

RNA molecules are single-stranded, but different types of RNA can readily form double-stranded sections like DNA. RNA is unique among the molecules in living systems, having the potential to store information like DNA and the ability to catalyze chemical reactions like proteins.

RNA, with a structural arrangement similar to DNA, has the potential to store information. This is most easily recognized in some viruses that use RNA as a primary information storage molecule. However, RNA is not used as the sole information storage molecule in any plant, animal, or microbial living system. There are several types of RNA with many functions in the cell. Most of these functions are involved in making proteins (protein synthesis).

RNA can also catalyze a few chemical reactions. After RNA is produced, or transcribed, from the information in DNA, it is "edited" into a final product that has the information necessary for making a specific protein. Some of the editing process is catalyzed by RNA molecules called ribozymes. Ribozymes cut and splice RNA molecules during editing, but they are not capable of replicating themselves or transcribing information into proteins like DNA can. Another catalytic activity for RNA is found in ribosomes. Ribosomes are made of protein and RNA. The RNA portion of a ribosome catalyzes the formation of peptide bonds to make proteins from amino acid subunits. Other proteins in the ribosome help position the RNA and amino acids to allow the reaction to take place. Ribosomes and ribozymes typically have additional proteins present during their catalytic reactions. Proteins assist by stabilizing or positioning the RNA catalyst.

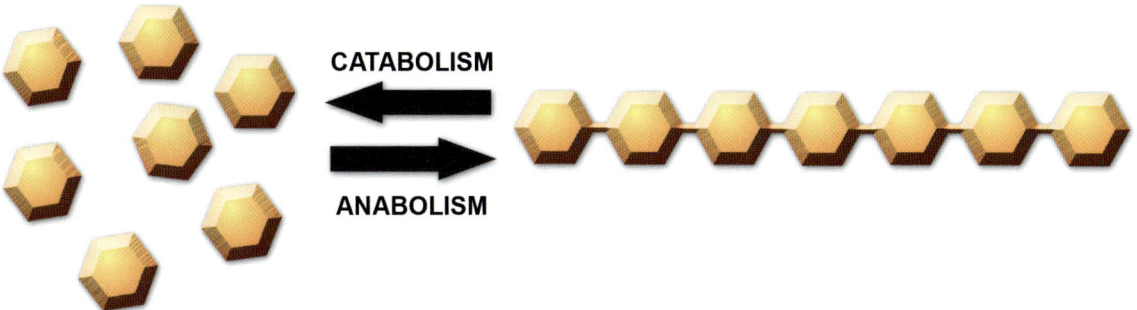

Metabolism is the sum of all chemical reactions. Anabolism makes larger molecules, such as proteins, from smaller subunits, such as amino acids. Catabolism breaks down larger molecules into smaller ones. Digestion of food into nutrients is an example of catabolism.

Metabolic Cycles are Characteristic of Life

Metabolism is the sum of all the chemical reactions that take place in the cells of living things. Metabolism includes reactions that make large molecules from smaller subunits (anabolism) and reactions that break down large molecules into smaller subunits (catabolism). The synthesis of proteins from amino acid subunits is an example of an anabolic reaction, while the digestion of starch into its subunits, sugars, is an example of catabolism. Typically, the assembling of a large molecule from smaller subunits requires energy to be added to the reaction. The breakdown of a large molecule, such as starch into sugars, typically releases energy. Enzymes catalyze these reactions and DNA has the information for their regulation and control.

Many metabolic systems, or pathways, in cells use what are called metabolic intermediates. Metabolic intermediates can be made from proteins, fats, or sugars (carbohydrates) and are recycled through a pathway and used repeatedly. To illustrate this, consider the following hypothetical pathway. Substance A is converted to substance B by losing atoms and electrons to make product 1. Substance B is converted to substance C by also losing atoms and electrons, which are used to make product 2. Substances C and D are combined to produce substance A and the process can repeat itself. The products of the metabolic cycle can be used to produce energy or make a substance needed by the cell. Many metabolic intermediates are small molecules with 2-6 carbon atoms combined with hydrogen and oxygen. Losing or gaining the equivalent of a water molecule (H_2O) or carbon dioxide (CO_2), or simply rearranging the atoms in a molecule, converts these molecules into the next metabolic intermediate.

Origin of Life

One of the best understood metabolic cycles is the Kreb's cycle, or citric acid cycle. In this cycle, a six-carbon citrate molecule (substance A) is eventually converted to a five-carbon molecule (substance B), accompanied by the loss of a CO_2 molecule and electrons (product 1) from citrate. This five-carbon molecule is eventually converted into a four-carbon oxaloacetate (substance C), again with the loss of a CO_2 molecule and electrons. Oxaloacetate (substance C) combines with a two-carbon acetyl molecule (substance D) to form citrate (substance A) and the cycle continues. The purpose of this cycle is to produce electrons that can be used to assemble an energy molecule called adenosine triphosphate (ATP). The source of the additional carbons in the acetyl molecule (substance D) comes from the catabolism of sugars or fats. The CO_2 molecules lost in the cycle are the waste products from the catabolism of sugars or fats.

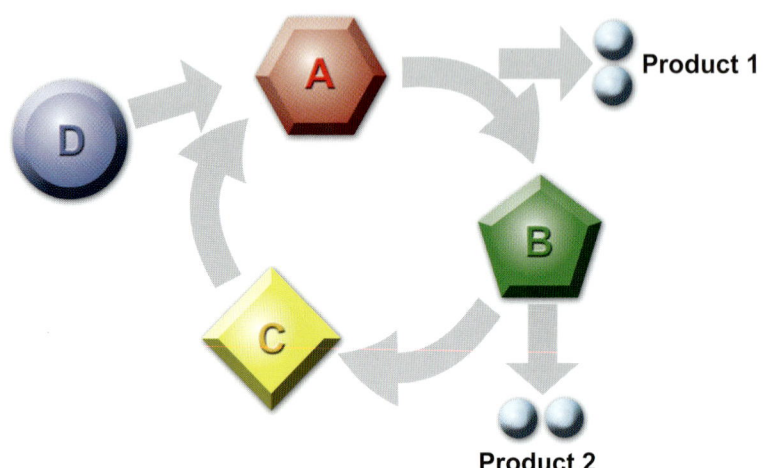

An illustration of metabolic cycles. Substance A is converted into substance B by losing atoms and electrons (product 1). Substance B is converted to substance C by losing atoms and electrons (product 2). Substances C and D combine to form substance A.

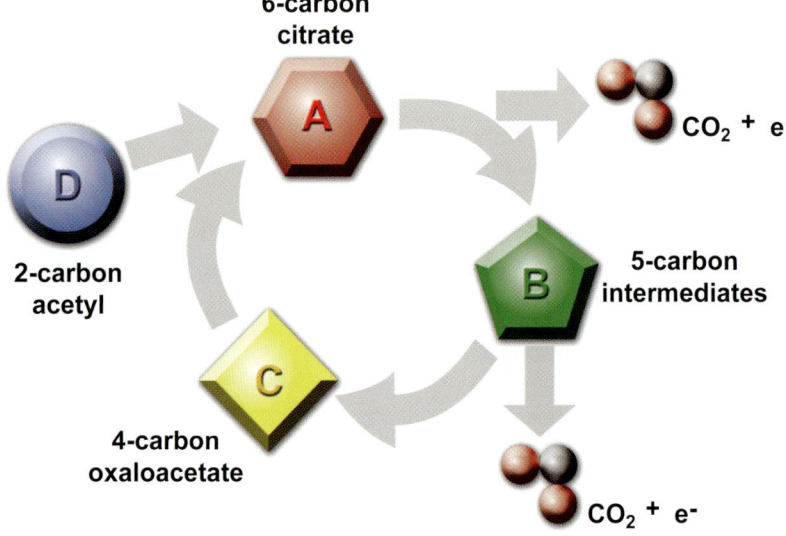

A simplification of the citric acid cycle. Citric acid is converted to a five-carbon substance by losing atoms and electrons. The five-carbon substance is converted to a four-carbon substance by losing carbon dioxide and electrons. A four-carbon substance, oxaloacetate, combines with a two-carbon acetyl molecule to form citric acid, and the cycle continues. Carbon dioxide is a waste product and the electrons will be used to produce an energy molecule, ATP.

ATP is the energy molecule that is used by the cells of living things in many chemical reactions. ATP is similar to the nucleotides in DNA and RNA, having a base (adenine) and sugar, but it has three phosphates instead of one. Guanosine triphosphate (GTP) is also an energy source and is structured just like ATP, with three phosphates and a sugar bonded to the base guanine. The reactions that form proteins from amino acids, copy or replicate DNA, and transcribe RNA from DNA all require ATP and GTP for energy. Without these energy molecules produced from metabolism, the synthesis of proteins and the activities of DNA would not be possible. ATP and GTP provide just the right amount of energy required for reactions in the cell. These molecules must be present with proteins and nucleic acids to make life possible.

Creating Life in the Laboratory

We observe that life is cyclical. Which came first, the chicken or the egg? The observable life cycle of the chicken does not have a starting or stopping point. Chickens lay eggs that develop into chickens that lay eggs. All living things go through a life cycle. These life cycles fit the creation account, which records the creation of living things fully formed and able to reproduce after their own kind. The life cycle started from a living source—the Creator.

The same is true of the chemical systems that make life possible. The chemistry of living things also involves many cycles, one of which is called the "central dogma." The central dogma was named by Francis Crick, one of the discoverers of the structure of DNA. The central dogma is the recognition that DNA requires proteins to replicate and to transcribe RNA to make proteins. We could add to this that ATP is also necessary for DNA replication and transcription, and DNA is necessary to make ATP for these activities. Like the chicken and egg example, DNA, RNA, proteins, and ATP are involved in a cycle that requires all of them to be available at the same time for life to exist. These substances make movement, growth and reproduction, response, and the use of energy possible for all living things. The role of DNA, providing information, is dependent on the role of the enzymes that provide catalysts to make the expression of information possible. The expression of information from DNA, through a catalyst, is dependent on energy-producing molecules. Just like some animals are dependent on specific plants for food, single chemical processes that make life possible are also dependent on other chemical processes. This dependency or interrelationship of living systems and living things is a characteristic of life that was created at the beginning.

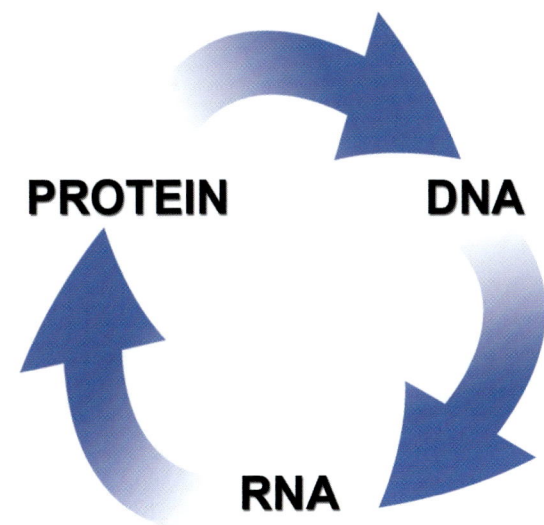

The central dogma. DNA transcribes RNA to make proteins that are needed by DNA to transcribe RNA.

Many scientists reject the concept that life was created and have investigated various possibilities for how life could have come into existence from nonliving materials. If life came from a nonliving source, then which life-giving molecules were the first to form? DNA has the ability to pass the information of life on to the next generation and to regulate and control the activities of cells through the production of proteins. DNA, however, has no catalytic activities, and the double-stranded structure of DNA makes it far too complex to be a feasible candidate for the first molecule of life. Furthermore, DNA is dependent on proteins for replication and transcription. RNA has a few catalytic properties and has the potential to store information, but it cannot provide a source of energy to accomplish all these activities alone. RNA does have a self-catalytic property that enables it to catalyze reactions on itself, but RNA cannot replicate itself or transcribe the production of proteins needed by living systems. Proteins have catalytic functions that make life possible, but they lack an information storage system. The amino acid subunits of proteins are the least complex molecules involved in the central dogma, making them more likely to form by natural processes. ATP lacks information storage abilities, and although it is an energy source in the cell, it is not the catalyst for life-giving reactions.

AMINO ACIDS IN THE PREBIOTIC SOUP

In the 1930s Soviet biochemist Alexander Ivanovich Oparin hypothesized that the earth once had an ocean with the elements necessary to form the first molecules of life, popularly referred to as the "prebiotic soup theory." He included in his theory that sunlight or electrical sparks from lightning could have provided the energy necessary to form life-giving molecules. He also speculated that the earth had an atmosphere similar to that found on Saturn and Jupiter, with hydrogen, ammonia, methane, and little or no free oxygen. Although Oparin wasn't the first to propose the origin of life from the ocean (the Greek philosophers Anaximander and Thales also believed that life came from the ocean), his hypothesis is the inspiration for prebiotic experiments and space exploration looking for signs of life today.

In 1953, Stanley Miller devised an experiment to test Oparin's hypothesis that a prebiotic soup without the presence of free oxygen could produce the molecules necessary for life. Miller set up an apparatus designed to circulate the gases hypothesized to be present on a primitive earth past an electrical spark to form amino acids. Miller used methane (CH_4), ammonia (NH_3), and hydrogen (H_2), gases commonly found in the solar system on planets and moons. The gases were mixed with boiling water (H_2O) in a flask and circulated past electrodes that provided the energy necessary to combine the gases into amino acids and other substances. The products were condensed by a cold water trap for removal and verification. Miller was successful in producing

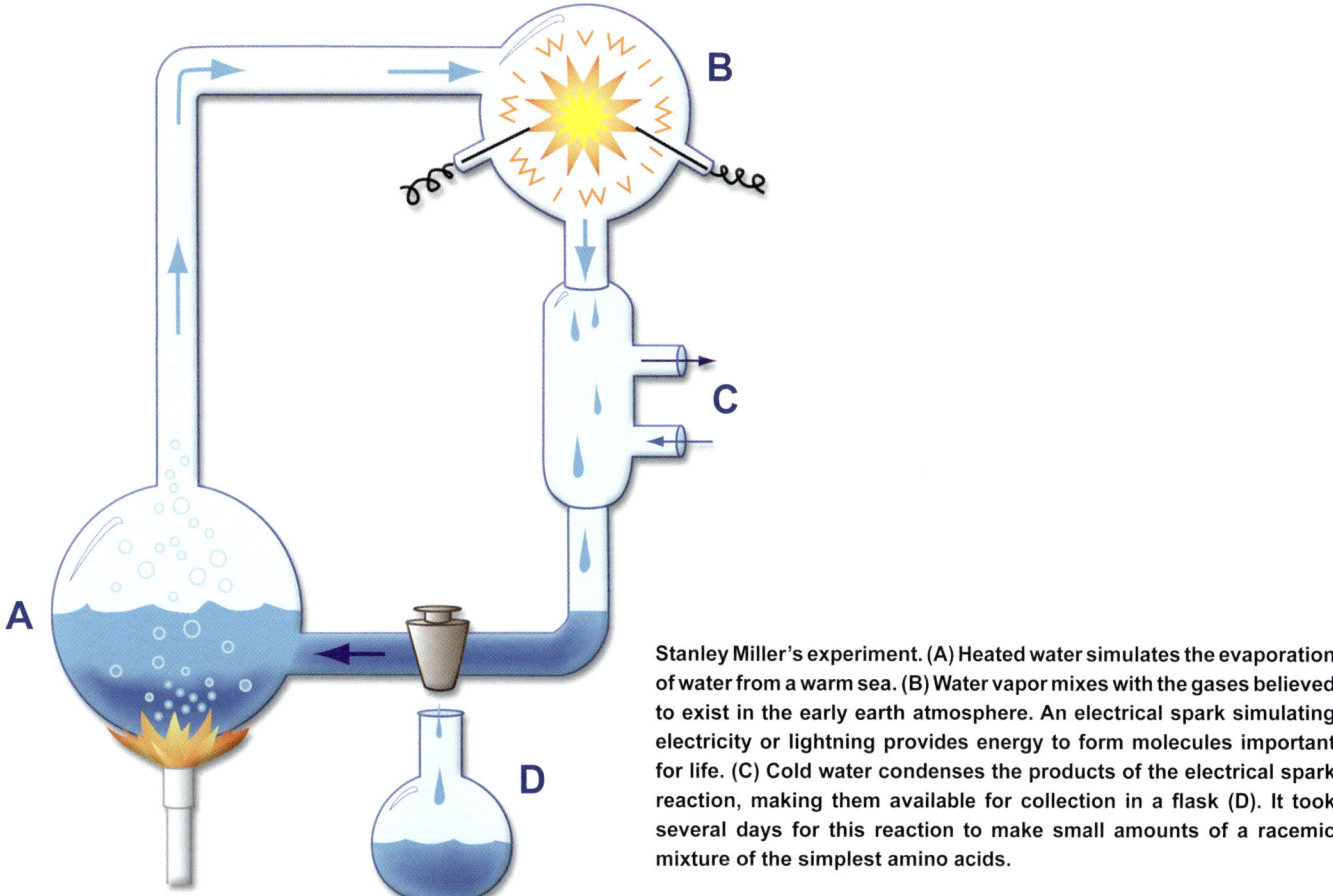

Stanley Miller's experiment. (A) Heated water simulates the evaporation of water from a warm sea. (B) Water vapor mixes with the gases believed to exist in the early earth atmosphere. An electrical spark simulating electricity or lightning provides energy to form molecules important for life. (C) Cold water condenses the products of the electrical spark reaction, making them available for collection in a flask (D). It took several days for this reaction to make small amounts of a racemic mixture of the simplest amino acids.

several amino acids found in living things, including glycine and alanine. Twenty years later, Miller's laboratory repeated the experiment using more advanced technology that allowed the scientists to identify and measure the quantities of several more amino acids.

The second experiment was a good match for the type and quantity of amino acids discovered in the Murchison meteorite found in Australia. The presence of amino acids in an object from space, and the laboratory experiment performed by Stanley Miller, independently confirmed that amino acids can be formed from nonliving systems. However, these amino acids do not match the type of amino acids found in living things. The Miller experiments and the Murchison meteorite both have nearly equal amounts of left- and right-handed amino acids. When a substance is made of equal amounts of left- and right-handed amino acids, it is called a racemic mixture. A racemic mixture of amino acids cannot form the proteins necessary for life. Nonliving sources of amino acids are characterized by these racemic mixtures. Amino acids from living sources are characterized by chirality, having only left-handed versions of the appropriate amino acids. The natural processes that formed amino acids in Miller's experiment and in the Murchison meteorite provide evidence that amino acids can be made by processes apart from living things, but only living things have the information to make only left-handed amino acids.

Miller's experiment also assumed that a hypothetical early earth had a

ORIGIN OF LIFE

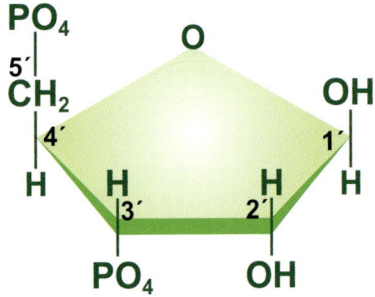

Ribose 3′, 5′-O-diphosphate. This contains a ring-shaped sugar called ribose, with each carbon numbered. Each carbon is designated with a prime to distinguish it from the numbered carbon atoms in the nitrogen base. In nucleotides, this ribose bonds with phosphates at carbons 3′ and 5′. Ribose from abiotic experiments frequently bond to phosphates at 2′ and 4′, inhibiting the formation of nucleic acids.

reducing atmosphere that lacked oxygen, a condition that is certainly not observable today. A reducing atmosphere is able to convert a substance like carbon dioxide (CO_2) into a compound that includes hydrogen, such as formaldehyde (CH_2O). These substances include the three atoms (carbon, hydrogen, oxygen) necessary for all biological molecules. An atmosphere with oxygen has the opposite effect, driving reactions away from biologically important molecules. The Miller experiments will not produce amino acids in the presence of free oxygen. There is little evidence that the earth ever had a reducing atmosphere. There is geologic evidence that the earliest sedimentary rocks were deposited during a time when there was a considerable amount of oxygen in the atmosphere, indicating that the earth has always had an oxidizing atmosphere. The lack of evidence for a reducing atmosphere, the need for only left-handed amino acids in living systems, and the inability of proteins to store information, have led many scientists to look elsewhere for the first molecules of life.

"The RNA World"

The discovery that some RNA molecules have catalytic activities, coupled with RNA's potential to store information, moved these molecules to the "front of the line" in the search for earth's first biologically significant molecules. If an RNA molecule could catalyze its own reactions and store information for the next generation of molecules, then the "chicken and egg" problem would be partially solved. The theory that RNA was the first biologically significant molecule to appear on the earth was termed the "RNA world" by physicist and biochemist Walter Gilbert in 1986. The RNA world depicts an earth that once had a completely RNA-based form of life devoid of the presence of amino acids or DNA.

The challenge to the RNA world for scientists is to show how the complex nucleotides in RNA could have been produced by nonliving (abiotic) processes. This involves the formation of the sugar ribose, the four different bases, the addition of a phosphate group, and the assembly of all three components into RNA nucleotides. Just like Miller's synthesis of amino acids, the components of RNA would have had to come from a prebiotic soup of molecules that are commonly found in the solar system. Several of the molecules used in the prebiotic synthesis of RNA would have included formaldehyde (CH_2O), hydrogen cyanide (HCN), and ammonia (NH_3), to name a few.

The five-carbon sugar ribose found in RNA nucleotides is a right-handed molecule that has been difficult to produce abiotically in the laboratory. Scientists have literally had "mixed" results in their attempts to form the correct ribose sugar. Many reactions result in mixtures of different kinds of ribose sugars, including many left-handed sugars. In addition, the five-carbon ribose in RNA bonds to the phosphate backbone at the ribose carbons numbered three (3′) and five (5′). In attempts to make RNA ribose, many of the resulting ribose sugars formed phosphate bonds at carbons two (2′) and four (4′) instead of carbons three and five. Furthermore, the kind of ribose found in RNA nucleotides was typically a minor part of the products of these reactions. When the correct ribose is formed, it decays at a rate too quickly to make it a feasible reactant in the prebiotic synthesis of RNA nucleotides. The reactions that are able to produce small quantities of RNA ribose require concentrations of reactants that are too high for an assumed prebiotic ocean.

The formation of RNA bases from a prebiotic soup has also proved to be troublesome. There are four nucleotide bases in RNA: adenine, guanine, uracil, and cytosine. There is a feasible pathway for the formation of adenine from hydrogen cyanide (HCN) and ammonia (NH_3), however, the concentration of hydrogen cyanide necessary for the reaction is far too high to be realistic in a prebiotic ocean, and there is no evidence that the earth had an atmosphere with ammonia. Because of this, a few scientists have suggested that adenine arrived on the earth from meteorites, while others have suggested that the reactants to form adenine were concentrated in lagoons or in ice. Cytosine has been successfully made through prebiotic synthesis reactions, and uracil is formed by the hydrolysis (a reaction that adds a water molecule) of cytosine. This reaction provides only two of the four bases necessary for RNA synthesis.

Although there has been some success forming the sugar ribose suitable for RNA and two of the bases in RNA, assembling these components into nucleotides has been met with little success. Even starting with RNA ribose and the bases cytosine and uracil, the synthesis of nucleotides with either cytosine or uracil has not been achieved under prebiotic conditions.

Just like the prebiotic synthesis in Miller's experiment yielded a racemic mixture of amino acids, prebiotic synthesis of any nucleotide also yields a variety of left- and right-handed molecules. The sugars and nucleotides of RNA in living systems are both right-handed molecules, and prebiotic experiments do not produce solely right-handed sugars or nucleotides.

The problems involved in forming RNA nucleotides from prebiotic sources have led to speculations of a pre-RNA world. The theory of a pre-RNA world assumes that there were precursor molecules that gave rise to RNA. Because of the problems with forming the correct ribose sugar, it has been suggested that a pre-RNA polymer called peptide nucleic acid (PNA) contained amino acids in place of the sugar-phosphate backbone of RNA. In this molecule, a polymer is made from amino acids bonded together to form the backbone, with RNA (or DNA) bases bonded to the chain of amino acids. Another substitute for the RNA sugar ribose is a five-carbon sugar that has the same atomic structure as RNA ribose, but it has a different shape. This polymer is called pyranosyl RNA (p-RNA). While both of these substances can be formed in the laboratory, none of them have ever been observed in living systems, and how they would have been transformed into the RNA observed today is unknown. Instead of "life as we know it," any living system based on PNA or p-RNA would constitute a form of life that we have never observed, or "life as we don't know it"! The problems with a pre-RNA world are so immense that one scientist, Nobel Laureate Christian de Duve, stated that life based on the pre-RNA world is dependent on "miracles" and outside the realm of science.

The Metabolism First Hypothesis

What if the complex molecules of RNA or amino acids were not the first molecules that made life possible? What if the first molecules were simple two- or three-carbon molecules organized into chemical cycles that performed a variety of energy-producing chemical reactions? From these simple chemical cycles, the energy could hypothetically be produced to eventually generate a catalytic and information system. The hypothesis that these small carbon molecules, involved in metabolic cycles, were the first molecules of life is sometimes called the "Metabolism First" hypothesis or the theory of "Self-Organizing Biochemical Cycles." Remember, metabolism is the sum of all chemical reactions that take place in living organisms. Many metabolic reactions use small carbon compounds and are cyclical, regenerating the molecules in each cycle. The hypothesis is based on the need for an energy source to drive the organization of not only a metabolic cycle, but also the formation of information and catalytic systems. These metabolic cycles must be coupled to a system that releases energy to produce the molecules necessary to make life.

The Metabolism First hypothesis is based almost entirely on theory. There have been a few experiments performed that show how carbon dioxide or carbon monoxide could be reduced (added electrons and hydrogen) to precursors of life-giving molecules that have carbon, hydrogen, and oxygen. However, there is no experimental evidence that a number of these types of reactions would self-organize into a set of reactions that would make life possible. Leslie Orgel, a prominent prebiotic origin-of-life scientist, stated that the idea that these reactions could organize into a set of reactions similar to a metabolic cycle "appeals to magic."

Does Life Exist Somewhere Else in the Solar System?

Is there life on Mars? In 1996, television and newspapers reported that NASA scientist Dave McKay found a bacterium-like fossil in a meteorite recovered from Antarctica and presumed to have originated from Mars. McKay's evidence was presented in the August 1996 edition of *Science* magazine, one of the premier scientific journals in the world. Did McKay really find evidence for life on Mars, or was there another explanation for the object in the Martian meteorite? Is it possible that life exists on other planets and moons in the solar system? Titan, one of the moons orbiting Saturn, is nearly as large as Mars and has a thick atmosphere consisting mostly of nitrogen (N_2) and methane (CH_4). Could the atmosphere on Titan harbor life-giving molecules and provide clues for how life began on earth? NASA and the European Space Agency have financed several missions to Mars and the moons of Saturn to find answers.

Life on Mars?

The possibility of life on Mars has captured people's imaginations since dark lines were first observed on its surface. In the first half of the twentieth century, astronomer Percival Lowell popularized the theory that the dark lines represented canals carrying water to Martian oases from the polar ice caps. The belief that the dark lines were canal systems wasn't completely disproved until 1965, when images taken by a spacecraft, Mariner 4, of Mars' surface showed no signs of the proposed canals. The dark lines have since been demonstrated to be an optical illusion observed from the surface of the earth. Although Mars was shown to have no evidence of intelligent life similar to humans, the hope of other more "primitive" life forms continued.

One of the first missions to Mars was a project that sent two Viking landers to the planet's surface in 1976. Both landers had several instruments on board to collect information about Mars, including cameras that were able to take pictures of the Martian surface. The landers performed several tests, including experiments to detect the activity of living systems in the soil. At first scientists believed they had a positive result for life from the Viking tests. But after careful analysis, it was determined that the chemistry they observed in the Martian soil was a result of physical processes that were not related to life. Most scientists concluded that there was no life on Mars based on the results of the Viking experiments.

There are many obstacles for life to thrive, or even exist as inactive

MARS

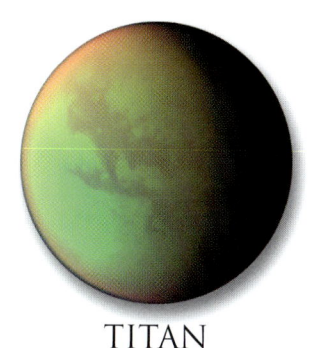

TITAN

Image Credit: NASA

ORIGIN OF LIFE

A Viking lander on the surface of Mars.
Image Credit: NASA

forms, on Mars. Mars lacks many of the life-giving features of earth. Unlike the nitrogen/oxygen rich atmosphere on earth, Mars has an atmosphere consisting mostly of carbon dioxide, lacking any of the significant oxygen needed by living things. Not only is the atmosphere all wrong, it is too thin, resulting in air pressure too low for liquid water to be sustained on the surface. If water was released from below the surface of Mars, it would instantly vaporize and form ice crystals due to the low atmospheric pressure and low temperatures.

Liquid water is a necessity for life. On earth, there is an abundant supply of water to support life. For life to exist on any other solar system body, liquid water has to be present at least some of the time. Water in the form of ice is a common substance in our solar system, even outside of the earth, so it should be no surprise that water ice is present on Mars. Water ice in small quantities was detected in the soil by the Phoenix Mars Lander in 2008 and was observed condensed on the Viking landers in 1976. How much water ice is on Mars is still not completely understood, but the existence of water ice in the soil located on the Martian Arctic Plain (North Pole) and in the atmosphere has encouraged scientists to keep looking for the possibility of life under the surface of Mars. If water ice exists there, scientists believe that underground heat sources might melt the ice and make it available for living things. Even if liquid water can be verified someplace on Mars, however, other problems seem insurmountable for life to exist there.

Differences abound between Mars and earth. The earth is protected by a robust magnetic field, blocking harmful radiation that would destroy life. Mars, however, does not have a strong magnetic field, and its surface is bombarded with radiation that would eventually kill all life forms found on earth. If living things on Mars were able to hide in the soil to escape the radiation, they would have trouble finding nutrients. Mars has soil that is highly oxidizing. This soil chemistry destroys nutrients in much the same way that an oxidizing atmosphere would have prevented the formation of amino acids in the Stanley Miller experiment. Nutrients consisting of carbon, hydrogen, and oxygen would be oxidized into carbon dioxide and water—waste products of metabolism—removing the potential for any nutrient to last long enough to provide living things with the energy to sustain life.

We know from studying life on earth that many living things, such as certain types of bacteria, can survive by making food using inorganic (without carbon) sources for energy instead of the sun. Some of these organisms live deep in the ocean and start food chains by using the energy available from the reaction of hydrogen sulfide and iron sulfide. These are the types of organisms that scientists predict might be able to survive on Mars. This is why Dave McKay thought he discovered a type of bacteria in the meteorite sample believed to be from Mars. Bacteria that can survive harsh conditions are the types of living things scientists speculate would be found on Mars today or in the distant past. Unfortunately for McKay and other scientists looking for life on Mars, the "fossil" was later identified as an artifact caused by the process of preparing samples for viewing under an electron microscope. Ten years after his "discovery," few scientists believe that the sample was the fossil of a living thing.

Many spacecraft have been sent to Mars to look for conditions that would support life, and many experiments have been conducted on its surface to look for signs of life. As of 2008, two rovers and the Phoenix Lander were still looking for signs of water on Mars, and more missions are planned. As yet, there is still no direct evidence that life could exist or ever has existed on Mars.

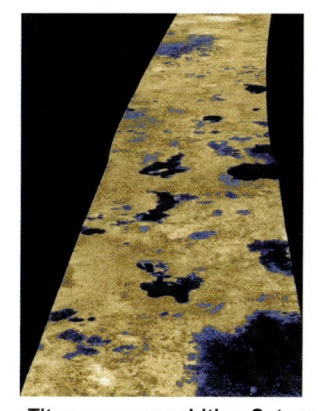

Titan, a moon orbiting Saturn, has lakes, pictured on the left, formed by the precipitation of ethane and methane. The lakes on Titan produce a dark image similar to the lakes on earth that are formed from water.
Image Credit: NASA

ORIGIN OF LIFE

STANLEY MILLER'S CHEMISTRY ON TITAN

Is there a place in the solar system that might provide the proposed conditions for how life or its precursor might have formed on earth? Scientists believe the answer to this is yes. Titan, a large moon orbiting Saturn, has a thick atmosphere with some of the substances necessary for the formation of molecules important for life. The atmosphere on Titan is mostly nitrogen (N_2), with a little methane (CH_4) and traces of other hydrocarbons such as ethane (C_2H_6). No molecules produced by living things have been detected on Titan, but laboratory experiments have produced some interesting results that scientists have considered possible on Titan. Tholins (a variety of molecules formed from hydrocarbons and nitrogen) have been detected on Titan. These molecules are considered by some to be possible precursors to the chemistry of life. Tholins are complex carbon compounds able to combine with water to form molecules that are believed to have existed on a primitive earth. However, there are problems with the formation on Titan of molecules important to life. Titan is extremely cold and liquid water has not been detected on this moon, although there is evidence that a liquid of some kind lies underneath the surface. The Cassini orbiter passed by Titan more than 40 times between 2004 and 2008 and recorded surface features that had moved more than 19 miles. This is good evidence that the surface is floating on a liquid substrate. This liquid substrate might not be water produced from a subsurface heat source, though. It could be liquid hydrocarbons similar to those identified on the surface. Titan has a liquid cycle in which methane and ethane precipitate out of the atmosphere and collect in lakes and small

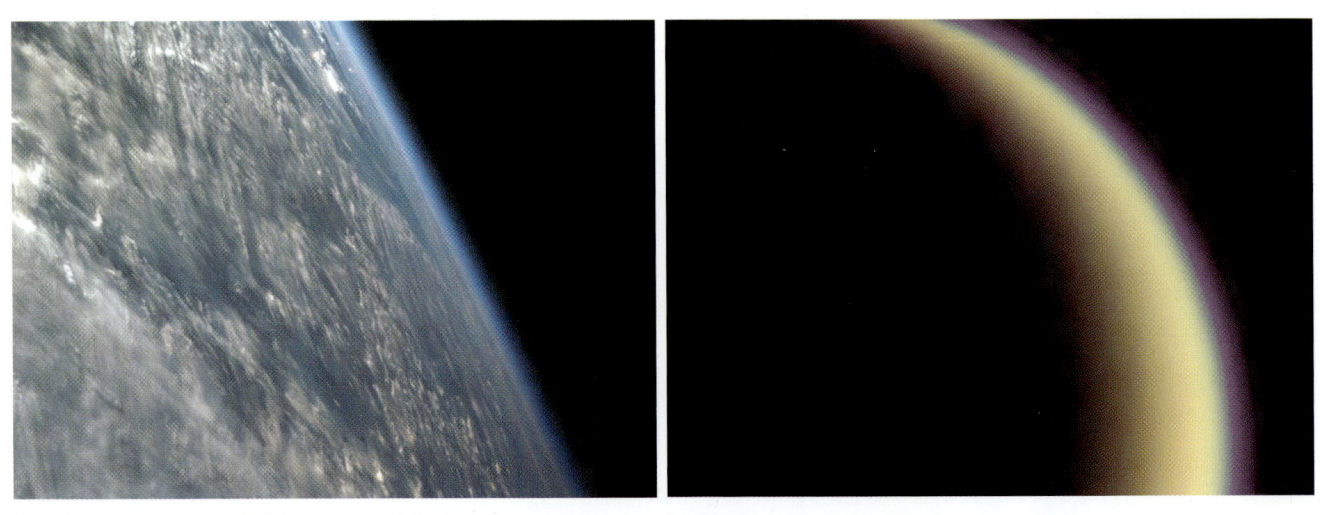

Earth's atmosphere (left). Titan has a thick atmosphere of nitrogen and hydrocarbons (right).
Image Credit: NASA

seas on the surface. This liquid cycle does not involve water, but it is the only other liquid cycle in the solar system besides the water cycle found on earth. This could be the source of the subsurface liquid responsible for the observed shift of surface features on Titan.

The formation of molecules similar to those found in living systems requires a source of liquid water, as Stanley Miller showed in his experiments. Tholins, found in the atmosphere on Titan, are considered a strong possible precursor for molecules found in living systems. Tholins are formed from methane and ammonia by exposing them to an electrical spark in the laboratory, using a method similar to Miller's. On Titan, an electric source of energy is unlikely and the most plausible source of tholins is from UV photolysis. Some of the tholins formed from UV photolysis in the laboratory are hydrocarbons that do not react with water, and these are the tholins that look like haze in Titan's atmosphere. The inability to react with water would make the formation of life-giving molecules difficult, if not impossible.

Tholins made from electrical spark experiments were able to react with the oxygen in water to form amino acids. Amino acids, formed from Titan-type tholins in the laboratory, made a racemic mixture of molecules similar to the ones produced in Stanley Miller's experiments simulating an early earth. Again, the formation of amino acids from nonliving sources produced molecules characteristic of nonliving reactions.

THE PURPOSE OF CREATION

Scientists continue to investigate how life could have originated on earth from nonliving sources. Laboratory experiments have failed to produce a consensus among scientists concerning which molecules first enabled life to get started. Some scientists favor amino acids as the first molecules, while others believe in an information-first system, such as the RNA world hypothesis. Others believe that metabolism was the first biochemical system to appear on the earth. Still others believe that the conditions for the beginning of life were never possible on earth, and life had to be transplanted from another place in the universe. Although some progress has been made since Miller's 1953 origin-of-life experiment, each hypothesis has many problems remaining, prompting scientists to admit that some origin-of-life scenarios require "miracles." Even if all the molecules important for life were assembled in the laboratory from nonliving sources, scientists would still have to accept by faith that the process they identified was how life came into existence on the earth. Since no one was around to observe where life came from, and life does not come from nonliving material today, scientists would have to accept by faith that their laboratory experiments have identified how life developed from nonliving material.

Scientists might one day manufacture a cell in the laboratory with all of the chemistry necessary for life. Artificial proteins, chromosomes, and cell membranes have already been made, and many other substances necessary for life can be obtained from living systems in a variety of ways. These systems might be able to replicate or perform some of the functions that living things do, mimicking some of the attributes of life. Since plant life and living cells were created from the elements of the earth, producing a facsimile of this type of life might be possible for scientists, to a limited degree. Advancements in robotics and computers, frequently called "artificial life," will also contribute to how science defines life. These new discoveries will lead to modifications of the scientific definition of life. Science has consistently struggled with defining life based on what life is perceived to be. New definitions of life will be given as more is learned about creation and how to manipulate it.

However, the creation of life as we know it requires an act of God. Remember, having only a partial definition of life that does not include all facets of what living things are will lead to identifying nonliving things as life and possibly misidentifying living things as nonlife. It is certainly possible that humans will be able to manufacture systems in the laboratory that appear to have the qualities of life, when all that has been accomplished is a set of chemical reactions that obey the laws of physics God has established for the natural world.

The earth was created to be inhabited, and it has all the requirements necessary for life. Life was also created to be interdependent. That is, all life forms have a role or function that affects other life forms in the environment. Life was not created just for the sake of producing a living thing to exist alone in an environment. God created plants and the microbial organisms to provide food for animals and humans. That is their purpose in creation. Humans and animals were created to glorify their Creator. Man was created to have fellowship with his Creator and to serve Him and his fellow man. Each part of creation is interrelated to the other parts of creation. This includes chemical pathways in living systems, the relationships between organisms in an ecosystem, and the relationship creation has with the Creator. There is purpose for everything that has been created. This does not support the notion that isolated forms of life could exist on Mars or the moons of Saturn with little or no interaction with other life forms. The other planets and moons of the solar system were not created to be inhabited. These solar system bodies lack the basic necessities for living things, such as liquid water and a water cycle, protection from radiation, ecosystems that sustain a variety of organisms, a carbon cycle, and a nitrogen/oxygen atmosphere. The other planets of the solar system were likely created to tell time and record seasons. It is also possible, by their presence, that they help support life systems on earth. This would be their purpose in creation.

We observe that life comes from similar pre-existing life, a process termed biogenesis. We observe that all living things need coordinated relationships for life to be sustained. We recognize significant differences in the "activities" of plants, animals, and humans—differences due to the separate creation events for each kind of life. The observations made about life direct us back to the impossibility of life from nonliving material and the recognition that life requires a Creator.

BIBLIOGRAPHY

Austin, S. A. 1982. Did the Early Earth Have a Reducing Atmosphere? *Acts & Facts*. 11 (7).

Bradley, J. P. et al. 1997. No 'nanofossils' in martian meteorite. *Nature*. 390 (6659): 454-456.

Brown, R. H. et al. 2008. The identification of liquid ethane in Titan's Ontario Lacus. *Nature*. 454 (7204): 607-610.

Campbell, N. A. and J. B. Reece. 2005. *Biology*, 7th ed. San Francisco: Pearson, Benjamin Cummings.

Cockell, C. S. et al. 2000. The Ultraviolet Environment of Mars: Biological Implications Past, Present, and Future. *Icarus*. 146 (2): 343-359.

Davis, J. J. 1975. *Paradise to Prison: Studies in Genesis*. Grand Rapids, MI: Baker Book House.

Garrett, R. H. and C. M. Grisham. 1999. *Biochemistry*, 2nd ed. Orlando: Harcourt Brace College.

Gilbert, W. 1986. Origin of Life: The RNA world. *Nature*. 319 (6055): 618.

Joyce, G. F. 2002. The antiquity of RNA-based evolution. *Nature*. 418 (6894): 214-221.

Kvenvolden, K. et al. 1970. Evidence for Extraterrestrial Amino-acids and Hydrocarbons in the Murchison Meteorite. *Nature*. 228 (5275): 923-926.

Larralde, R., M. P. Robertson and S. L. Miller. 1995. Rates of decomposition of ribose and other sugars: implications for chemical evolution. *Proceedings of the National Academy of Sciences*. 92 (18): 8158-8160.

Lowell, P. 1895. *Mars*. Boston: Houghton, Mifflin and Company.

Margulis, L. et al. 1979. The Viking mission: Implications for life on Mars. *Journal of Molecular Evolution*. 14 (1-3): 223-232.

McKay, D. S. et al. 1996. Search for Past Life on Mars: Possible Relic Biogenic Activity in Martian Meteorite ALH84001. *Science*. 273 (5277): 924-930.

Miller, S. L. 1953. A Production of Amino Acids Under Possible Primitive Earth Conditions. *Science*. 117 (3046): 528-529.

Minkoff, E. C. 1983. *Evolutionary Biology*. Reading, MA: Addison-Wesley.

Morris, H. M. 1976. *The Genesis Record*. Grand Rapids, MI: Baker Book House.

Neish, C. D. et al. 2008. Rate Measurements of the Hydrolysis of Complex Organic Macromolecules in Cold Aqueous Solutions: Implications for Prebiotic Chemistry on the Early Earth and Titan. *Astrobiology*. 8 (2): 273-287.

Nelson, D. L. and M. M. Cox. 2005. *Lehninger Principles of Biochemistry*, 4th ed. New York: W. H. Freeman.

Niemann, H. B. et al. 2005. The abundances of constituents of Titan's atmosphere from the GCMS instrument on the Huygens probe. *Nature*. 438 (7069): 779-784.

Oparin, A. I. 1938. *The Origin of Life*. New York: MacMillan.

Opik, E. J. 1966. The Martian Surface. *Science*. 153 (3733): 255-265.

Orgel, L. E. 2000. Self-organizing biochemical cycles. *Proceedings of the National Academy of Sciences*. 97 (23): 12503-12507.

Orgel, L. E. 2004. Prebiotic Chemistry and the Origin of the RNA World. *Critical Reviews in Biochemistry and Molecular Biology*. 39 (2): 99-123.

Ring, D. et al. 1972. Prebiotic Synthesis of Hydrophobic and Protein Amino Acids. *Proceedings of the National Academy of Sciences*. 69 (3): 765-768.

Robinson, R. 2005. Jump-Starting a Cellular World: Investigating the Origin of Life, from Soup to Networks. *PLoS Biology*. 3 (11): e396.

Shapiro, R. 2007. A Simpler Origin for Life. *Scientific American*. 296 (6): 46-53.

Soffen, G. A. 1976. Scientific Results of the Viking Missions. *Science*. 194 (4271): 1274-1276.

Stofan, E. R. et al. 2007. The lakes of Titan. *Nature*. 445 (7123): 61-64.

Wachtershauser, G. 1990. Evolution of the first metabolic cycles. *Proceedings of the National Academy of Sciences*. 87 (1): 200-204.

Waite, Jr., J. H. et al. 2007. The Process of Tholin Formation in Titan's Upper Atmosphere. *Science*. 316 (5826): 870-875.

Watson, J. D. and F. H. C. Crick. 1953. The Structure of DNA. *Cold Spring Harbor Symposia Quantitative Biology*. 18: 123-131.

Yen, A. S. et al. 2000. Evidence That the Reactivity of the Martian Soil Is Due to Superoxide Ions. *Science*. 289 (5486): 1909-1912.

For More Information

Sign up for ICR's FREE publications!

Our monthly *Acts & Facts* magazine offers fascinating articles and current information on creation, evolution, and more. Our quarterly *Days of Praise* booklet provides daily devotionals—real biblical "meat"—to strengthen and encourage the Christian witness.

To subscribe, call 800.337.0375 or mail your address information to the address below. Or sign up online at www.icr.org.

Visit ICR online

ICR.org offers a wealth of resources and information on scientific creationism and biblical worldview issues.

- ✓ Read our daily news postings on today's hottest science topics
- ✓ Explore the Evidence for Creation
- ✓ Investigate our graduate and professional education programs
- ✓ Dive into our archive of 40 years of scientific articles
- ✓ Listen to current and past radio programs
- ✓ Order creation science materials online
- ✓ And more!

For a free Resource Guide, contact:

Institute for Creation Research

P. O. Box 59029
Dallas, TX 75229
800.337.0375